THE ENGLISH AND THEIR COUNTRY

THOMAS BURKE

First published by The British Council c.1944

First published in this format in 2016 by IWM,
Lambeth Road, London SE1 6HZ

ISBN 978-1-904897-48-4

A catalogue record for this book is available from the British Library.
Printed and bound in the UK by Gomer Press

Image p20 © Harold White

Every effort has been made to contact all copyright holders.
The publishers will be glad to make good in future editions
any error or omissions brought to their attention.

FSC
www.fsc.org
MIX
Paper from
responsible sources
FSC® C114687

THE
ENGLISH
AND THEIR
COUNTRY

FOR OVERSEAS FORCES

THOMAS BURKE

English people shopping in the market of a small town

THE ENGLISH
AND THEIR COUNTRY

The English have for centuries been a puzzle to the people of other countries, and the failure to solve the puzzle has led the stranger to use all sorts of epithets. The English have been called mad, hypocritical, impossible, ridiculous, cunning, simple, and many other terms that, taken together, cancel each other out. Yet there is perhaps some justification for this bewilderment and these confused attempts to clarify it. The English are peculiar, and their island is, in its physical features, climate, history and products, like no other territory of equal size.

The English are a compound of the characteristics of many other peoples. In English blood run the strains of many races. There were the Early Britons with a civilization of their own. Then came the Romans who overthrew that civilization and for four hundred years substituted the Roman way of life. Then the Romans withdrew, and in came the Danes and the Saxons. Then came the Norman-French. Each of these invaders left something with us. None of them really "conquered" England. They mixed with the people they found here, and England absorbed them and made them part of itself, so that to-day the English are a little of everything of western Europe, and the characteristics of the various races may be seen in the faces and structure of the people to this day. In the south-western county of Cornwall you find the shorter descendants of the Iberians. In the south-east you find the stocky Roman type; in the east and north-east the tall, fair Scandinavian, and in other districts the sturdy Norman type.

As the country absorbed these racial characteristics, so

it absorbed foreign culture, adapted it, and made it English. It drew from all sources.

Its early architecture it took from France, Italy and the Gothic North. It drew its fashions in dress at different times from Italy, France and Spain. It has a strong, rich literature which in spirit is wholly English, and in substance as varied as the national character, but it took its forms wherever it found them. Its early ballad form it took from Provencal troubadours. It took the sonnet from Italy, the satire from ancient Rome, the essay from France, the novel from Spain.

Even the landscape of this little island, about half the size of the American State of Texas, reflects something of

6

all Europe. No other island, indeed, can show such variety of landscape. In a triangular territory of less than 60,000 square miles you find miniature Alps, miniature Danubes and Volgas, miniature fjords, miniature marshes, miniature steppes, miniature deserts, and miniature forests. At every fifty miles or so the landscape changes, and in one day you may pass through scenery reminiscent of Dutch, Swiss, Italian, Scandinavian, and French landscapes. From the ugliest industrial districts you pass in fifteen minutes into the most rural and pastoral scenes. Ten miles from one of our most modern business centres you may come to a town whose cathedral is mediaeval, whose streets have the unspoiled beauty of the sixteenth century, where the

Hills (in the South-West)

Plains (in the East)

The second
largest chemical
works in the
world

noise of industry is never heard, and where life seems to slumber in century-old repose. You may breakfast in a town founded by the Romans, such as Colchester, and lunch in Boston and think yourself in Holland. These varieties of scene have led to equal varieties of social and economic life.

Outside the towns, however blackened they may be by the stains of industry, all the country is green. That is one of the first points remarked by most visitors – the greenness of England. It is the heritage of our abused climate. Never at any time is the weather of this little island the same in all parts. On one day you may have snow in Hampshire, while in Cornwall you have daffodils in bloom and palms growing in the open. You may have thick fog in a town, and twelve

miles away brilliant sunshine. Sometimes in one small corner the weather changes three or four times a day from warm to cold, and from rain to sun, and back again. Englishmen and their visitors make bitter complaint about the caprice of the English climate, but it is this caprice which helps to give the country its green mantle, its variety of scenery, and its variety of human temper. That is why English people talk so much about the weather, why English novels make so many allusions to it; its frequent change affects not only the physical scene but the human psychology and human reactions to circumstance.

These varieties—of weather, landscape, and racial strains—together help to make the many

Durham's 800 years' old cathedral

varieties of English character. There is a basic English character, but in different districts it runs into fine shapes and shades peculiar to those districts. As the people of the north, south, east, west and midlands differ in physical appearance, so they differ in moral qualities. Each district in this island has its recognizable type with its own local characteristics and eccentricities. Thus, the men of one part of England will be noted for their closeness with money, while the men of another are noted for their free spending. In one county you will find the people taciturn and cautious; in the next county warm-hearted and hospitable. In one place you will find them surly and pessimistic, and fifty miles away you will find a people buoyant and easy-going.

Busi
man

With a little experience you will know, by looking at the landscape, what to expect. The spirit and manner of a people is made by the spirit of the landscape and the nature of the soil with which they live. The Fen country of Lincolnshire is a melancholy, damp country; the observant

Steel-worker

Farm-worker

Engine-driver

Taxi-driver

traveller therefore will not expect to find lighthearted people with laughter in their eyes; he will be prepared for people in tune with their landscape. In the western counties we find rich soil and generous sunshine, and so we find people with rich red faces and kindly voices; while in the south-western extremity the iron rocks of Cornwall and the fierce gales that beat upon its coast produce the hardy but saturnine Cornishman.

The different counties offer even further varieties of scene and mood. In Devonshire the earth is red. In the adjoining counties it is brown, and, in the midlands, black. In the south the fields and lanes are fenced with hawthorn hedges. In the north the fences are piles of flat stones. In other parts they are hurdles or wired palings, or mud and flint. Not only are the landscape and the soil peculiar to each; the very style of building of the older towns and villages is local.

Three studies in harmony

Before the days of easy transport all building was done with whatever material was nearest to hand, so that the buildings of these older spots have the air not of having been built but of having grown out of the soil—as in one sense they have. They are in complete harmony with their natural surroundings; as perfectly placed in their setting as the trees and hills about them. Thus, the cottages of eastern England are built of timber and flint—flint being a local product. Placed elsewhere, they would strike a false note, but on their own ground they fit with the contours and belong to the scene. Again, in Gloucestershire the houses are built of the local yellow-grey stone, in a tradition which has developed for three thousand years, and nothing but this stone will harmonize with those hills and fields. In Cambridgeshire again, they are built of the local white brick; in Lancashire of red brick; in Cornwall of granite; and they melt so well into the landscape that they seem to have been there from the beginning of time. In the south and west the cottages are of stone with thatched roofs; in Warwickshire of black timber and white plaster; and in some of the more remote hamlets you may even find cottages built as the Saxons built them of wattle and daub-sticks and hardened mud.

These minor differences of neighbouring scenes resolve themselves into one broad and major distinction of the people of this island. Here, as in much larger countries, there is a sharp difference between North and South. Roughly one may say that the north and northern midlands of England are its industrial area, and the south the pastoral. Only roughly, since much farming is done in the northern counties, and the south has many manufacturing centres. But generally the distinction stands. Our ships, most of our coal, our iron, our steel, our clothes, come mainly from the north; our food from the south. The distinction applies also to character. In many countries the people of the North are generally harder, more energetic, of simpler tastes than their fellows of the South; and so it is in England. The North cultivates the elementary qualities, the sterner virtues; the South refines upon them and cultivates the graces of life. The people of the English North are blunt of speech and manner. They say what they mean, even if it offends, and they act without regard to the more fastidious courtesies. They call it honesty. The South calls it uncouth. The

The Pastoral South

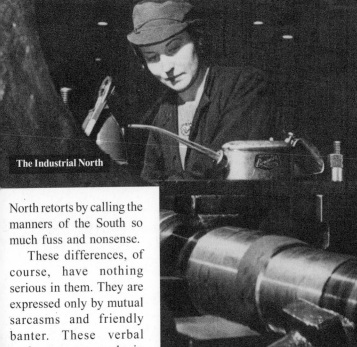

The Industrial North

North retorts by calling the manners of the South so much fuss and nonsense.

These differences, of course, have nothing serious in them. They are expressed only by mutual sarcasms and friendly banter. These verbal exchanges are made in other parts; even adjacent counties give each other satirical nicknames marking each other's surface differences and registering amusement at each other's oddities of speech. Each county of this little island has its local dialect rooted in the remote past, and many of the pleasantries turn on this matter. All the people speak English, but they speak it in such different ways that the peasant from Cornwall can hardly understand the peasant of eastern England, and the shepherd from the rugged valleys of the Lake District in the north-west can hardly talk to the shepherd from the smooth, rolling hills of Sussex in the south, while the Londoner on holiday has difficulty in understanding any of them.

Marked differences of character and other matters exist also between the English on the one side, and their neighbours, the Welsh and the Scots, on the other. Wales and Scotland, divided from England by impalpable frontiers, are, in physical features, moral characteristics and speech, separate nations. Few Englishmen can appreciate as a Scot does the poems of Scotland's national poet, Robert Burns; the English indeed cannot even understand them without a glossary, so different is Scots speech from English; while that portion of Welsh literature written in Welsh, and the Welsh poetic festivals called Eisteddfods, are, of course, complete mysteries to the English. But both countries are partners, with Northern Ireland, in the United Kingdom; Wales since the end of the thirteenth century, and Scotland since the beginning of the eighteenth. All four countries are governed under one Crown, and represented in the English Parliament, and the people of these countries, with their distinct manners and customs, and their sarcasms against each other, live together in a humorously-tolerant union, and when danger threatens any part of this island its people show that they are indeed a united kingdom; all are British.

To try to give in these few pages a clear analysis of the English character would be to try to do what many volumes have not succeeded in doing. Scores of books have been written both by Englishmen themselves and by men of other countries, attempting to resolve that English psychology which so puzzles the stranger. None of them has accomplished its quest, and one of them, published a few years before the present war by a European observer of our ways, expressed the difficult nature of the quest in its title: "The English'—Are They Human?"

The most frequent criticism of the Englishman made by men of many different countries, turns on his frigidity and

The village inn

stiffness; a criticism that surprises the Englishman since he is not aware of anything in himself that warrants it. But one can see that to more volatile people his outward reserve would give an impression of a chilly and insubstantial temperament, and no indication of the rich warm character that it covers. The English countryman is even more reserved than his fellow of the towns. Enter a village inn, and the company of farmers and workers will ignore you. Address them, and you will get a word in reply; no more. Ask them questions, and they will answer in monosyllables, non-committally. They will volunteer nothing, and you will have no free talk with them

Her Majesty, Queen Elizabeth, talks to shipyard workers

until they have known you for some weeks and have learned who you are, where you come from, and what you are doing in their village.

But that reserve is surface only. It is a covering assumed by the Englishman to conceal the fact that he is fundamentally shy. Yes—shy. That may surprise those who see him as an arrogant pioneer and blustering adventurer who has built an Empire scattered over the seven seas. But it is true. Old as the English people are, the individual Englishman is always much of a boy with a boy's characteristics. Thus, far from being frigid and stiff, he is highly emotional, and at the same time ashamed of showing emotion. He is keenly sensitive, but his training has taught him that to be too sensitive is to be weak. He is naturally warm-hearted and at the same time afraid of being betrayed into what he thinks the vulgarity of exuberance. He wants to be liked, but will never show that

Concentration. When not playing dominoes these men handle railway engines

The spirit of the Army—at a football match

he wants to be liked. Far from being the hard-headed John Bull drawn by his own cartoonists, he is in truth sentimental. That is, he bases his conclusions more upon feeling than upon logic. Many of his views he finds it impossible to defend intellectually, yet he is sure he is right. He does things not because they are expedient but because he feels that in the circumstances they are the right things to do. Ask him why, and he cannot put his feeling into words. Argue with him, and show him by reason that the right thing is some other course, and he will still follow his own notion of right. It is something he knows not in his mind but in his bones and his blood.

But he will not admit to being guided by sentiment, and so he goes about in armour, and in the presence of strangers he seldom relaxes and lays it aside. Even with other Englishmen he wears it. He doesn't readily engage in talk in railway trains, restaurants or hotels. He wants to know something about a man before he knows him. He is shy of mixing with types outside his "set." He wants to be sure that the other man is his "sort," sharing the same tastes and manners; and he is embarrassed if he finds he has invited to his home a man who isn't of his "sort." When he does eventually lay aside his armour, then you meet the real Englishman—genial, generous, and sympathetically adaptable. He does not, like the men of some warmer countries, scatter his friendship freely to all who come along, but when he does give it he gives it with all his heart.

Another criticism, arising from this attitude of reserve, is that he is self-complacent and indifferent to opinion. That is a mis-reading. He is not perhaps, when he has made up his mind on a question, much influenced by outside opinion, but he is highly sensitive to his own criticism of himself, and, contrary to the stranger's belief, that criticism is going on all the time. He is never satisfied with himself, but he will not make that confession to strangers. Hence the attitude that gives the false impression of self-complacence.

Another trait of his that puzzles the stranger is that of treating flippantly all that is most serious and most dear to him. Courage, loyalty, sacrifice, his own country, the English way of life, the English flag, his personal honesty—all these matters, close as they are to his inmost heart, he belittles in his public talk and makes the objects of his laughter. Verbal expressions of patriotism, of heroism, of sentiment, are things he abhors, and whenever they happen in his presence he is embarrassed, and may hide his embarrassment by mocking them. Yet he is as patriotic, as heroic, as sentimental as anybody. Personal praise of himself, his achievements, or of things concerning him makes him as awkward as the boy he really is. His adored children he calls "the brats." His flag he calls "the duster." An overwhelming victory is "not a bad show." He is outwardly serious

only about trifles—about cricket, football, racing, stamp-collecting, gardening, golf, his dog, his car.

He has a great heritage of literature and art, and publicly he ignores it. He is little given to celebrating or even talking of the great intellectual figures of his country. Where English towns have statues they are usually statues of some admiral or general, or some local mayor or philanthropist; seldom of the son of that town who has made a figure in England's intellectual life. English streets are not named like those of some European countries, after poets, novelists, artists, philosophers; mostly they are named after the men who built them or the men whose land they are built upon. Huge editions of the works of the standard English writers are sold every year, but you would have to know an Englishman very well before you learned that he was familiar with them. It is all part of the perplexing English way of showing no pride in the things one can really be proud of; all part of the English reserve.

Deep in his nature is a strong vein of poetry; yet he will not openly claim it. He allows himself instead to be represented to

Cricket is one of the things that matter to the average Englishman

Perhaps a poet planned these houses

the world as a plain, bluff John Bull, shopkeeper, when he is in truth a Romantic, a creature of imagination and fancy. Look at the names he has given to his wild flowers—snowdrop, meadowsweet, love-in-a-mist, forget-me-not, shepherd's-purse, creeping-jenny, traveller's joy, snapdragon, London Pride. And the names he has given to his villages—Sleeping Green, New Delight, Nether Wallop, Huish Champflower, Nymphsfield, High Easter, Redmarley d'Abitot, Tiptoe, Orcheston St. George. And the fantastic signs he has given to his country inns—the Man in the Moon, the Puss-in-Boots, the Flaming Log, the Peaceful Home, the Merry Month of May, the Civil Usage, Bel and the Dragon. No plain John Bull would have bothered to invent those names. Yet the Englishman will continue to deny that he is given to fantasy, and continue to pass himself off as a plain practical man with no nonsense about him.

And, for that matter, there is a measure of truth in his claim. When his imagination is gripped by the romance of exploration, for example, or of scientific discovery or engineering achievement, he seldom rests content with fantasy alone. This is not to imply that he thereupon ceases to be a Romantic. On the contrary, it is his abiding sense of romance, even in seemingly commonplace everyday things, that spurs him on to practical effort. It is indeed in this spirit that the great English explorers, from Sir Walter Raleigh to Sir Ernest Shackleton, have set out into the unknown on their voyages of discovery. It is thus that scientists like Michael Faraday, who discovered magneto-electricity, and engineering pioneers like Sir Charles Parsons, who invented the steam turbine, have been impelled to turn fancy into fact.

Another of the many features of English life that puzzles the stranger is the number of "classes" into which the social scene is divided. We have the Peerage, the County, the upper-middle class, the middle-middle class, the lower-middle class, and the working class; each with its own manners and

But a practical man built these flats

customs, its own forms of speech and its own outlook on life. The largest of all these classes is the lower-middle class or *petit bourgeoisie*. It is the largest class in all western countries, and if the stranger wants to find the common denominator of a country's life it is that class, not the select well-to-do minority, whose way of life he must examine. It is mainly a town class. The life of the countryman is much the same in all countries. The differences between nations and their way of life is perceived mainly in their town life, and the life of this large class in England is in many aspects sharply different from that of the *petit bourgeoisie* of other countries.

From reading our novels, and from seeing our plays and films, the stranger may get the idea that the average Englishman is educated at one of our expensive schools called Public Schools—Eton, Harrow, Winchester or schools of that sort—and at Oxford or Cambridge; that he lives in a comfortable house attended by servants; that he is a member of a well-known London club; that he dines at expensive restaurants; that he hunts the fox and shoots grouse and pheasant; that his children have bright nurseries and are attended by nurses; that he takes his vacations among the resorts of Europe, or on a yacht, or by visits to the large country houses of his own country. It is not so. Only a very small percentage of the English people live like that.

The average Englishman, the representative, that is, of the great majority of our 45,000,000 population, does none of these things. The average Englishman is educated at a free school run by his County Council. At fifteen he leaves school and starts to earn his living as clerk, shop assistant, mechanic, country labourer. He usually lives outside the town in which he works in a little six-roomed house in a street of a hundred exactly similar houses. The house has no servants; it is run entirely by his wife and children. He is not a member of any well-known club. His "club", if he has any, is the local public-house. He does not hunt or shoot. His interest in sport is expressed by reading about it and by watching it at football matches, cricket matches, boxing matches, and by betting on horse races and greyhound races. He does not take extended vacations in Europe. All the months of the year, excepting one fortnight spent at an English seaside town, are given to work. He does not dress for his evening meal, and he does not take sherry or cocktail before dinner, or wine with the meal. He takes either beer or tea.

Some features of the life ot this average Englishman are, as I say, very English and are found in no other country. For example, the English breakfast. No other country begins the day with such a meal as porridge, eggs and bacon or fish or sausages, toast and marmalade and tea. And no other country knows the average Englishman's Sunday midday dinner of roast joint of beef or mutton, with vegetables, followed by an equally solid sweet, and succeeded by an afternoon sleep. And no other country

The fireside of an Englishman

knows the English Sunday and its penitential atmosphere. Sunday is the day when more people are at liberty to be out and about than on any day of the week. It is also the day when the perplexing English, instead of increasing their transport, reduce it, when they keep most of their restaurants shut, and when they restrict their public entertainment to music, except in those towns where cinemas are allowed to open. Perhaps that is why Americans who visited Europe in peace-time always felt more at home in the countries of the Continent than in England; the way of life was nearer to their own than England's.

Still, that is the English way. No Englishman can defend these illogical customs, and he doesn't try to. Though he suffers from them he doesn't get them altered. He prefers to suffer and exercise his privilege of grumbling. It is all part of his individualism. He wants to live his life with his family and cultivate his garden and follow his career with as little interference from or with others as possible. He is jealous of his privacy and it is part of his code to respect the

Home Guard training

SUNDAY AFTERNO

The boys are home on lea

After the week's work

It is very often like this!

ENGLAND

Walking in the mid-day sun

privacy of others. An English novelist, a friend of mine, was once entertaining some young men from another country. They were sitting in the garden when one of the young men asked: "Why do you English people have such high walls to your gardens? At home, our gardens have just little divisions, so that you can see all the gardens of the section on either side of you. What's the idea of these high walls?"

"Why," said my friend, "they're a feature of an Old English Custom known as Minding One's Own Business. We put up these walls to help us to do so."

Minding one's own business is a prominent feature of English behaviour; almost as prominent as "playing the game"—the English term for justice and for not taking advantage of another's weakness. The English have always had a passion not only for political liberty but for personal freedom. They have never liked being ordered about, and they do not in truth need to be. There is in every Englishman a sense of order, not imposed from without but grown from within, a heritage of centuries of freedom. This sense of order pervades all things English, and it goes, paradoxically, with the Englishman's intense individualism.

You may observe it not only in English life but in the English country scene. There you will find in operation the same sense of order, developed from centuries of loving and individual care. Almost all Englishmen are countrymen. Generations ago they came into the towns, but their roots are in the country, and the average Englishman's dream is to retire eventually to "a little place in the country," and to resume contact with the actual soil of England. It is this deep attachment of the whole people that gives to the English countryside its serene air of English well-being. No country has such orderly landscapes, such neat fields and hedgerows, such trim villages, such tidy farms, such demure rivers. This order is not the achievement of any political pressure or economic planning. It is an expression of the innate English sense of order translated from the individually self-ordered life of the people into the very face of England.

The English countryside is laid out in little parcels, each of them the product of personal effort, and it thus reflects the English character. The Englishman can be a good co-operator with his neighbours while still keeping his individualism. He is not willing to go beyond co-operation into the communal life, or to sink his individualism and be a State unit in a State home filled with State furniture. The average Englishman wants his own house, however small; his own little garden, his own dining-room and bathroom. He prefers the smallest and most inconvenient house and smallest patch of garden to the most up-to-date flat with an elegant garden common to all, a perfectly-fitted nursery common to all the children, and common tennis-court, swimming-pool, recreation-room. Superior as these amenities might be to anything he could

Landscape

personally afford, he would rather go without them so that he may live his own life in his own way, mind his own business, and enjoy a privacy in which others mind theirs.

It is this individualism, and the inconsistencies that go with it, that make him rather an enigma to the people of other countries. His logic, his values, are not theirs. You cannot tie him down to rigid formulae; you cannot be sure that in given circumstances he will behave thus and thus. He has always got a surprise, and is always surprised to find that he is in any way surprising. To himself his proceedings are eminently sensible, and indeed they are, so long as it is remembered that they are based on the logic not of reason but of feeling—not of prose but of poetry.

Englishman at home

City street in wet weather

Owing to limitations of paper supply, the British Council is issuing this booklet in this country solely for

OVERSEAS FORCES.

Booksellers, therefore, are supplied with it only on the understanding that it will not be sold to anyone except men and women in the uniforms of the Commonwealth, Empire, United States and other Allied Forces now visiting this country. It is hoped that members of the British Forces and the British public generally will appreciate that this account of English characteristics is intended for their guests.

Booklets on The SCOTS and their Country
The WELSH and their Country
The ULSTERMEN and their Country
are in preparation.

Published for
THE BRITISH COUNCIL
by LONGMANS GREEN & CO.
London   New York   Toronto

British Council Code Name—ENGANENG. Longmans' Code Number (1)00001.
Printed in England by The Sun Engraving Company, Limited, London and Watford.

Also from IWM Publishing

Victory In the Kitchen: Wartime Recipes

A collection of delightful and unusual recipes from the Second World War, showing the ingenuity and creativity behind dishes rustled up out of meagre rations – from austerity recipes such as scrap bread pudding, potato pastry and sheep's heart pie to hearty English favourites including Lancashire hot pot, Queen's Pudding and crumpets. With colour images of wartime posters throughout and an introduction by an IWM historian, this book is a fascinating look into what people ate in wartime.

978-1-904897-46-0
£6.99

Churchill's Cookbook

Churchill is well-known for his hearty appetite and love of food. This book gives a fascinating insight into what he ate during the Second World War, containing over 250 delicious recipes created by his personal cook, Georgina Landemare. From mouth-watering cakes, biscuits and puddings, to healthy salads and warming soups, it revives some forgotten British classics and traditional French fare – the food that sustained Churchill during his 'finest hour'.

978-1-904897-73-6
£9.99

Make Do and Mend

A delightful reminder of the techniques for household economies extolled by the wartime government. First published in 1943, all of the tips can be used to spruce up your wardrobe today. Old fashioned remedies for everything from washing silks and mending your clothes, to repelling the 'moth menace'!

978-1-904897-64-4
£4.99

Food for Thought: Keeping Well in Wartime

As relevant today as when they were first published in 1943, *Wise Eating in Wartime* and *How to Keep Well in Wartime* offer cheerful and practical advice on healthy diet, exercise and well-being. From providing a 'menu for the ideal meal' to addressing dilemmas such as 'do we eat too much sugar?', from offering useful remedies for fatigue to divulging frank advice on 'sex problems', these books give an intriguing insight into keeping well in wartime.

978-1-904897-76-7
£8.99